Keep Telling of Gaza

Khawla Badwan
Alison Phipps

Edited by Annick Yerem

Keep Telling of Gaza
Edited by Annick Yerem

Legal Notice. Annick Yerem has asserted her right under section 77 of the Copyright, Designs & Patents Act 1988 to be identified as the editor of this work. Khawla Badwan and Alison Phipps as authors reserve copyright to their work. Art work by Imad Abu Shtayyah. All Rights Reserved. No part of this book may be reproduced, stored in a retrieval system, or transmitted in any form, or by any means; electronic, mechanical, photopcopying, without prior permission from the editors/authors. However short extracts may be quoted on social media.

Published 2024 by Sidhe Press
https://sidhe-press.eu
Cover Art by Imad Abu Shtayyah

Also from Sídhe Press:

Our Own Coordinates
Poems About Dementia - An Anthology

The Crow Gods
Sarah Connor

Glisk and Glimmer
Poems About Light - An Anthology

Just One More Before I Go
Nikki Dudley

To Light The Trails
Poems About Women In A Violent World - An Anthology

Always Fire
Sarah Connor

Trigger warning:

Genocide

Dedication

For the Palestinian people, we keep telling.

For the children of the world, our words and wounds are part of the fight for a fairer future.

For all who tell the truth.

Contents

Dedication	iv
Foreword	viii
Introduction	x
3rd July	1
3rd July- Safe zones	2
14th July- The shipping	3
28th September	4
3rd October- When I die	5
14th September	6
9th August- Death Blocks	7
21st August	8
10th August- The bucket	9
2nd September	10
1st August- A world without order	11
14th July	12
18th August- Rice bag	13
3rd October	14
21st July- Ethics of love	15
28th September- Order.	17
29th August	18
26th August	20
9th July- The privilege	21
6th July	22
25th September- Under the Rubble	23
2nd September	24
26th September- call	25
15th August	26
12th July- Not Alone	27
21st July	28
6th October- Grow back	29
6th October	30
3rd September- To witness	31
25th August	32
2nd August- A kite over Gaza	33
5th September	34
14th September- Gasping	35
24th July	36
13th July- A sleepless child	37

18th July	38
3rd August- Once more	39
31st July	40
20th July- Justice	41
20th July	42
22nd July- Nothing but words	43
5th October	44
5th September- Unfreely	45
9th August	46
6th September- Undertaking	47
9th August	48
25th July- End of humanity	49
30th September	50
30th July- A child's head	51
6th September	53
27th July- A dad's letter	54
19th July- The sea.	55
7th August- Gaza sea.	56
12th July	57
28th July- A bombed school	58
19th August	*59*
23rd August- Death calls	60
17th August	61
24th August- Bread	62
20th September	63
5th August- Fire	64
22nd August	65
6th August- Scream	66
16th July	67
29th August- Lies of defence and security	68
28th September	69
31st August- Little brother	70
13th July	71
21st August- O Gaza	72
27th August	73
22nd August- Letdown	74
5th August	75
1st September- Gaza in September	76
2nd August	77
7th September- The Edge	78
8th September- In our millions	79

7th September	80
4th September- In memory of my brother's friend	82
9th Sep- Radical love	83
13th August	84
Shame is ours	84
26th August- Calls under bombs	85
11th September	86
10th September- Unjoinable	87
7th August	88
17th September	89
15th September- A curse	90
22nd September	91
11th September- No title	92
11th August	93
15th July- He can hear you	94
8th July	95
14th August- Birth certificates	96
13th September	97
15th August- Little one	98
23rd July- Dad's shoes	99
31st August	100
29th July- His face	101
11th July	102
2nd September- To try again	103
29th September	104
10th July- I cannot	105
23rd July	106
12th September- Teachers	107
4th August- Keep telling	109
19th September	110
4th July- To vote.	111
4th July	112
10th July	113
17th July- As I live	114
23rd September	115
7th October- A Year	116
7th October	117
Acknowlegements	119

Foreword

Poems are records you feel. They are conduits for *stepping in* – tuning frequency with other lives in ways no entry in a history book, no news article, no photograph, allows. This book passes a chain of word-torches, burning with horror and blessings, from a people who are being systematically, cruelly stripped of everything else —*'O! I have nothing / Nothing but words'*— to a humanity of readers outside, with no language to spit back ferocious love in the face of war. These poems are aware that in your care, they cannot die, cannot be stolen or buried, cannot be twisted less true. Cannot be erased. You hold in your hands absolute proof that the human spirit will make itself heard, even when every bird stops singing over the scorched earth. For the future children of Gaza, read every devastating word. Know them, share them, and keep them safe —until the time comes to place them back on the traumatised tongues of that future on the other side. *'Bless those who hold what remains / In their horror / In their rage / In their betrayal / In their grief... Bless the peace-makers / Bless the faith in the just world to come.'*

Ankh Spice – *The Water Engine*

"The French word *témoignage* is usually translated into English as bearing witness. It's also about testimony; a declaration of evidence. Many poets and artists talk about their role to observe society and humanity and to bear witness to its joys as well as its failings. But how to do that when we are witnessing such atrocities and inhumanity on an industrial and relentless scale, as have been inflicted on the people of Gaza and Palestine over the last 77 years.

Keep Telling Of Gaza bears witness to all the atrocity, injustice and inhumanity. It tells of the fear, anger, despair and grief of Palestinians murdered and mourning on a daily basis; it tells of the horrific inhumane acts of violence against the people of Gaza by the Israeli State. It tells us this in words written of in the moment, in the moment. It also tells us not to look away: to keep writing, to keep speaking up and, even in our own despair at not being able to stop or influence those that support or arm the oppressors, to keep bearing witness."

JP Seabright, writer, poet, editor

Introduction

In her instructions for living a life, the poet Mary Oliver, says:

Pay attention.

Be astonished.

Tell about it.

Thank you for choosing to pay attention, and to read our words about Gaza. Words, borne out of witnessing with grief, love, pain, and commitment. Words carrying wounds, screams, cries, flames, as well as literal descriptions from the livestreaming of death and destruction in Gaza. Words that offer the unspeakable, speaking up and breaking down in different forms of accountable witnessing.

Our words come, not from the great book of creation which was the muse for Mary Oliver's astonishment, but from Gaza, and from our own astonishment at the ease with which international laws have been destroyed in Gaza, from a determination to break the silence which has surrounded us from former friends, and colleagues who have chosen to do and say nothing.

We chose to follow the instructions for living a rich life, an honest life, a life that is compelled: and to tell about it.

This work is a project of digging words from underneath the rubble and between fires and flames. It attends to Gaza, speaks of Gaza, responds to Gaza, and disobeys the normalisation of what happens in Gaza. While we have nothing but words, we offer them to document one of the most horrific crimes known to humanity in modern history. Crimes in a land with a long history of dispossession in an iconic struggle, with injustices spanning across 77 years- and counting.

Mahmoud Darwish's poem 'Silence for Gaza' translated into English by Sinan Antoon, opens out the poetic space of Gaza:

They might implant tanks on the insides of its children and women. They might throw it into the sea, sand, or blood.

But it will not repeat lies and say "Yes" to invaders.

It will continue to explode.

It is neither death, nor suicide. It is Gaza's way of declaring that it deserves to live. It will continue to explode.

It is neither death, nor suicide. It is Gaza's way of declaring that it deserves to live[1].

Our documenting is a deliberate hand-fasting to truth telling, committed to the values, in Gaza, which as Darwish says, are 'different, different, different'.

The philosopher Hannah Arendt said, in Origins of Totalitarianism:

> *The totalitarian mass leaders based their propaganda on the correct psychological assumption that, under such conditions, one could make people believe the most fantastic statements one day, and trust that if the next day they were given irrefutable proof of their falsehood they would take refuge in cynicism; instead of deserting the leaders who had lied to them, they would protest that they had known all along that the statement was a lie and would admire the leaders for their superior tactical cleverness.*

We refuse to take refuge in cynicism. We refuse to settle with the commonly used sentence to refer to Gaza: there are no words left. We do not admire those who shred truth and profiteer from propaganda. We know the difference. We take it upon ourselves to find words even when

---

[1] https://mondoweiss.net/2012/11/mahmoud-darwish-silence-for-gaza/ last accessed 22nd October 2024

our words are fatigued, repeated, exhausted and overused. We refuse to state that we 'are so tired' but instead to find words every day. This is our task. We are workers with words. Many of our words amplify the cries of wailing mothers and fathers, screaming children, and horrified witnesses. As we sit with these horrors, we respond in poetic cries that are stunned and stunning. In dialogue over many months we have stunned each other, prompted each other, been a well of words for one another.

We invite you to read. We invite you to the explosion that is Gaza's truth.

Take your time to comprehend the enormity of the events in our poems.

Go easy on yourself if you struggle to make sense.

We, too, have found the task too daunting, beyond belief; too grave for any practice of sense-making. Nonetheless, as educators and scholars, we invite you to open your eyes and heart to learn more about the Gaza Genocide, to speak up and to keep telling of Gaza and the struggles endured by the Palestinian people.

These poems are in a constant dialogue with each other and Gaza. To mark authorship Khawla's are in regular script and Alison's in italics, bending in supplication.

We invite you tenderly back into truth. Into telling about it. And we offer you these words, as a way.

Who speaks for those without rights?

Tell us who.

3rd July

The wicked say MOVE.

We will destroy your neighbourhood.

We will destroy your refugee camp.

We will kill all your family.

We will destroy your schools.

We will destroy your universities.

We will destroy your food.

We will destroy the tents you now live in.

We will have no mercy.

3rd July - Safe zones

They declared some safe zones
Dropping leaflets of death maps
With colours and webs of lines

They declared some safe zones
Adding numbers to squares
With messages of death threats

Leave or else, they warn
Run or else, they threaten
Move or else, they abuse

Running to safe zones
Running in safe zones
Running from safe zones
Running out of safe zones

They engineered the death zones
People trapped between the lines
And bombs dropping everywhere

14th July- The shipping

They resumed the shipping of bombs

Smaller ones, they say, not the big bombs

Drop multiple ones to get the heavy bombs

Bomb

Bomb

They resumed the shipping of weapons

Raining death using all advanced weapons

Thinning a population with more weapons

Bomb

Bomb

They resumed the shipping of death

Their globally engineered death

Truly globalising- unlike any other death

Bomb

Bomb

They resumed the shipping of horrors

Bombing tents among endless horrors

A tiny strip of land witnessing all horrors

Bomb

Bomb

28th September

Give us more bombs,
demand The Wicked.
Ship them now.
Give us arms
for free.
We need to kill the children.
We need to kill.
We need to destroy the schools.
We need to flatten the homes
of the children
we are killing
and killing
and killing,

3rd October- When I die

When I die, reads a child's will.

Don't cry

This saddens me.

When I die,

Give my clothes away

To those in need.

When I die,

Send my accessories

To those names.

When I die,

Donate my allowance

Split it fairly.

When I die,

Look after my brother-

Says the letter under the rubble.

14th September

Bless the children

who want to play in the park

like normal children.

Bless the children

who want to learn in school

like normal children.

Bless the children

On pink roller skates

Comfort the fathers and mothers

Of the 16,500 children

killed by The Wicked. [2]

---

2 https://www.youtube.com/embed/7iwKiewWXdU

9th August- Death Blocks

They cut our bleeding land into blocks
Added numbers to mark the blocks
Splashed death between the blocks

They cut our bleeding land into blocks
Dropped leaflets as they bomb the blocks
Told the dying to leave the blocks

They cut our bleeding land into blocks
Nowhere else to go to between the blocks
The whole map is covered in red blocks

They cut our bleeding land into blocks
Trees witnessing the erasure of blocks
Birds refusing to sing over their blocks

21st August

We will say we are
going to cease fire
and when you start to hope
that there might
be an end to
holding bodies
and body parts in your arms
we will carry on as before
but force you to
agree to our one condition:
that you praise our forever war,
and call it peace.

Say The Wicked.

10th August- The bucket

And on the screaming screen

There were more crying men

Holding many pieces

Mixed with blood

With their eyes wide open

Their faces covered in dust

Digging more pieces

Placing them in a bucket

In a bombed school

Full of human pieces

And the bucket is full

Getting fuller

An old man shakes his hand

To the bucket he points

The bleeding bucket

The once white bucket

And in disbelief he says:

Show the bucket to the world

2nd September

We will not target military sites
say The Wicked.
We will kill thousands
and we will expel people;
all the people;
and when others follow rules of war and hit
our military bases
in revenge for our killing
we will unleash a hell on the world
like you never saw.

1st August- A world without order

Unstoppable evil

Flowing weapons

Endless killing

A standing ovation

Another journalist killed

Last seen above rubbles

Buried without a head

Brain cells mixed with sand

Fellow journalists mourning

Reporting in pain and tears

We won't stop, they say

Cracking voices in dismay

A population trapped

Starved in a death camp

Traumatised to death

There's nothing but grief

14th July

She is missing.
He is missing.
They are all missing.
They are trapped.
Their bodies are unreachable
under the rubble of home.
We cannot oil their skin in a final
touch of love, or dig their graves
and gentle them with our tears.
They are missing.

Missing. [3]

---

[3] https://www.theguardian.com/world/article/2024/jul/12/palestinians-missing-gaza-warfare-red-cross

18th August- Rice bag

I saw a child's remains in a rice bag

Shredded into nothing but three kilos

Placed in a rice bag that remains half empty

I saw a child's remains in a rice bag

O my little one! You were not buried whole

Remains, parts, pieces- like my witnessing heart

I saw a child's remains in a rice bag

O rice bag! What has become of us

Held by a father, digging humanity`s grave

3rd October

In future The Wicked
will wring their hands
and blame their false friends
who did not do as friends do
and stop their crazed, wanton
destruction. But as dealers do
feeding their violent habit,
profiteering.

21st July- Ethics of love

Existing for one another

Against their politics of hate

With the aesthetics of symbols:

A watermelon

A kuffiyeh

A poster

A sticker

A kite

A flag

A pin

Building a movement

Of love, solidarity, and collective struggle

With eyes meeting, tearing and comforting

In our thousands, the chant goes

In our millions, the crowd repeats

We are all Palestinians, the spirit echoes

Looking after one another

Holding our otherness and togetherness

Remaking life with ethics of love

18th September

Bless the question:
how many must die to
satisfy the false god of security?
How many children?
How many births must be prevented,
how many limbs amputated,
how many journalists assassinated,
how many homes turned to rubble?
How many pointless reminders about
redline lies?

Bless the questions
with just answers.

28th September- Order.

Order! Order, says the man

Asking for order in that big hall

As the world falls in a black hole

Order! Order, repeats the man

Speaking to Nations

Once called United Nations

Order! Order, shouts the man

As the crumbling unfolds

And nothing holds

Order! Order, then a criminal speaks

Bombs on buildings as he speaks

29th August

The Wicked destroy sewage systems,
ban cleaning products,
ban personal hygiene products,
enforce period poverty.
A bottle of low quality shampoo
costs £40.
A bar of soap
costs £10.
There is no soap for clothes or dishes.

No soap, say The Wicked.

No soap.

Bleed.

24th July- The Sky

The sky looked sad last night
Thick grey covering cosmic light

The air is heavy still
Gaza is under things that kill

I look at the sky and cry
Is it possible Gaza shares this sky?

I see children screaming in fear
Their eyes forever haunt me here

Don't stop speaking, they say
We're digging words, I say

26th August

In the city of date palms
–Deir al Balah–
the dates are turning from
red to yellow
ready for harvest.
The Wicked say
run for your lives
or we will murder the children
here too,
and we will destroy the groves
of dates
with our merciless, precision hate.

9th July- The privilege

Beware the other

They are inconveniently here

They don't count in your sphere

Turn around

Look away

Beware the other

Don't mention their dead

Don't care about their end

Turn around

Look away

Beware the other

If challenged, call it neutrality

Don't worry about morality

Turn around

Look away

Beware the other

Let's stand firmly together

Protecting our privilege forever

Turn around

Look away

6th July

Wait and watch.
See what is said now.
See what is done now,
which law is respected at the International Court,
which children are still for bombing and burning,
which genocide matters,
what is expended.
Watch and wait.
Wait and watch.

25th September- Under the Rubble

I saw a child

I saw lots of rubble

A child under the rubble

Gasping for air

Taking her last breath

I watch and weep

Endless streaming of horrors

Of shameful powers

Of crumbling humanity

Of laughter and applause

All under the rubble

2ⁿᵈ September

*Today we will vaccinate
against Polio again
say the good doctors.*

*Today The Wicked say they will
pause their killing long enough
for the immunisation to be
undertaken*

before they begin killing the immunised.

*Mercy is no longer merciful
in the land devastated by The Wicked.* [4]

---

[4] https://www.bbc.com/news/articles/c4gl62rvvp8o.amp

26th September- call

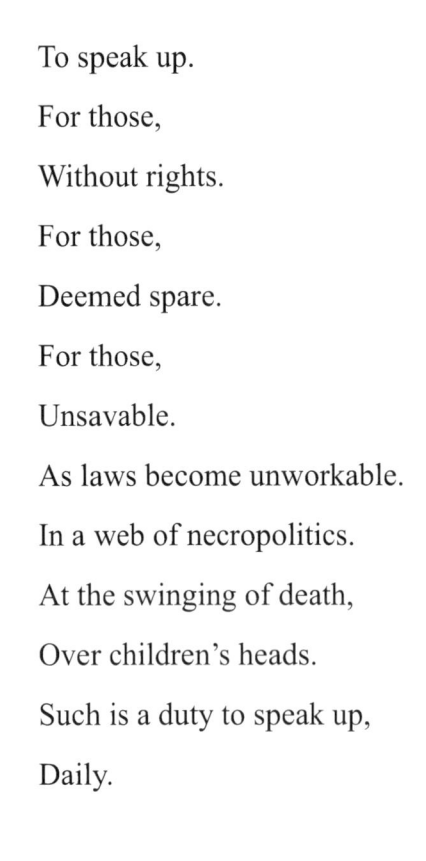

To speak up.

For those,

Without rights.

For those,

Deemed spare.

For those,

Unsavable.

As laws become unworkable.

In a web of necropolitics.

At the swinging of death,

Over children's heads.

Such is a duty to speak up,

Daily.

15th August

Bless the attempts,
however feeble,
to assert
with every fibre of being
that the mass murder of a people
by an occupying force
in the name of vengeance
is wrong.
Is always wrong.

12th July- Not Alone

As the world crumbles

As the grip gets tighter

As the space becomes smaller

As the walls keep popping up

As the norm is to be betrayed

As the voice continues to crack

As the tears refuse to dry

As the crowd go on as usual

You are not alone

You are not invisible

You are not a burden

In our thousands

In our millions

21st July

Praise those who teach life.
Praise those who illustrate the beauty.
Praise the Alphabet.
Praise those who tell children
of what was good
and wickedly destroyed.
Praise The A-Z of Gaza
Praise the books and the brushes.
Praise the good life that is remembered
and must be restituted and restored. [5]

---

5 https://buymeacoffee.com/ashrafhamad/e/278241

6th October - Grow back

Will my legs grow back?,

Asks a crying child in Gaza.

With fear on his face,

And sadness in his eyes.

Asking again.. looking at me.

Searching for a lost hope,

A promise of advanced medicine.

A miracle.

And I lose my eye contact.

My cheerful voice breaks down.

I see it shattered on the sandy road,

Under the scorching sun.

I look at the amputated legs,

Hiding my face away.

If only limbs can grow back.

I spot a football outside a tent.

How can I hide this thing?

I look at my legs,

His amputated legs.

I look at the sky,

The buzzing drones.

How far the bombs travelled?

Who sent them?

Who developed them?

Who paid for them?

And the world becomes a violent web.

And now, you.. you.. you

You have to respond:

Will his legs grow back?

6th October

Bless those days when we can't breathe
because every day is a day we cannot bear it.
The hypocrisy,
the double standards,
the law breaking,
the arrogant impunity,
the threats
the endless killing of kith and kin.
Bless the always unbearable days.

Withhold the luxury of despair.

3rd September- To witness

Houses on fire

Smoke in the air

Flames spreading

Bricks falling apart

Palm trees bending

A watch not moving

Birds refusing to sing

A witness with a camera

A child crying in the distance

An observer with a broken heart

Words bursting grief on the screen

Lines writing themselves in disbelief

Sounds piling up as screams happen

A genre of maddening mourning to witness

25th August

Blessed are the truth tellers.
They do not sugarcoat.
They speak in clinical facts.
They know every red line is crossed.
They do not have the slightest hope
any good can now be done.

They bravely give a steady terminal diagnosis.
They are not undone. [6]

---

6 https://x.com/middleeasteye/status/1827175900418576598?s=46

2nd August- A kite over Gaza

Flying a kite over Gaza

Bearing witness to what was

Mourning the state of what is

Screaming 'let Gazaaaaaa live'

Flying a kite over Gaza

Passing between deadly drones

Shivering with every explosion

Surviving clouds of toxic dust

Flying a kite over Gaza

Whispering salam to a dying child

Wishing salam upon Gaza's heart

Waving salam to a grieving land

5th September

*"If you gave me a button
to just erase Gaza,
every single living being in Gaza
would no longer be living tomorrow,
I would press it in a second,"
they say.*

*Of our blatant bravado and lust
to kill we will boast.
Of our wickedness there will be no end.* [7]

---

7 https://x.com/middleeasteye/status/1831038760521232571?s=46

14th September- Gasping

I can't breathe.

They sucked

The air, all light.

They enforced death

Heaviness, brutality.

They normalised

Horrors, crimes-

No end.

They destroyed

Life. All life

As we once

Knew it. Lived it.

Believed it.

I'm gasping for air.

Searching for life

In this eternal darkness.

And such is the learning

To live again,

Daily.

24th July

If you oppose our means of illegal annexation,
if you oppose our segregation,
if you say poliovirus is not a just dessert,
if you say children should not be murdered,
if you deliver humanitarian assistance,
we will vote to designate you terrorists.
We are that intent.
say The Wicked. [8]

---

[8] https://x.com/ajenglish/status/1815550636340978101?s=46

13th July- A sleepless child

Have you seen the sleepless child?

On the road she lies

Resting with no rest

Looking alive but lifeless

Exhausted with loss

New to loneliness

With an empty stomach

And no surviving family

Under drone-filled skies

Inhaling burned bodies

Witnessing the worst of humanity

Not looking anyone in the eye

Not looking you in the eye

She's just staring at the sky

18th July

*For the days where there is not
the slightest hope,
when the world looks away
again and again,
and the people are murdered
again and again,
and there is not the slightest hope
of ending the forever war
again and again.*

3rd August- Once more

Tell them once more, dear friend, once more
We lived a life full of love, pain and pride
We loved to live, lived to love and cried
We died in our thousands but we tried

Tell them once more, dear friend, once more
We hugged our children yet many died
We tried to teach hope facing a genocide
We cared for our trees with our arms wide

Tell them once more, dear friend, once more
We mourned our cities without losing our mind
We ate leaves, starved to death and sighed
We know death and its horrors we can't hide

Tell them once more, dear friend, once more
Say all these things combined
Pass our tales to your child
I write in tears yet I smiled

31ˢᵗ July

"The birds have stopped singing"
writes my friend.
"They have been silenced by the bombing
they hide and cannot be seen
in the trees
in quiet times they come in search of
water and food."
"The birds have stopped singing."
writes my friend.

20th July- Justice

In pursuit of justice
In the absence of justice
Amid the ruins of systems of justice
Comes the ruling from The Court of Justice

No longer up for debate
No longer 'complicated'
No longer 'impartiality'
No longer 'two sides'

It's illegal
It's apartheid
It's occupation
It's racial segregation

Affirming what we knew for years
Adding legal terms to our pain and fears
Confirming we aren't just mad in tears
Crying 'Free Palestine' across all spheres.

20th July

*Praise the truth tellers
for at last the judges have spoken.*

*An illegal annexation,
violent settlement of the land,
by what has become an
Apartheid State, say the judges.*

*Sharp cries of protest are
healing words as justice.
Bringing restitution
a vessel for peace.* [9]

---

9 https://www.icj-cij.org/sites/default/files/case-related/186/186-20240719-adv-01-00-en.pdf

22nd July- Nothing but words

Holding the crumbs of words

Putting them together to scream

Begging them to honour the loss

Hoping that they can bear the pain

O! the gift of words

O! the pain in words

Remaking life with words

From words, for more words

Wrapping arms around the lonely

Announcing they are not alone

Repeating we are not alone

Repeating we are not alone

Against the violence of silence

Against the erasure of words

O! I have nothing

Nothing but words

5th October

Bless the quiet quitters
who may not speak out
or protest,
who confess to not understanding
but who know what they
are seeing live-streamed
and hearing from leaders.
The ones who have thought about this
and talked about this,
and are done,
and will not spend their money
on any more blood.

5th September- Unfreely

To play unfreely

On broken roads

Under buzzing drones

Between desperate tents

To roll unfreely

With pink roller skates

Without any human rights

In a terrifying death camp

To fall unfreely

Murdered by monsters

Shot in cold blood

Covered in a sheet

And the world rolls on unfreely

9th August

For those facing the hardest decisions
after facing the hardest decisions,
as Israel bombs tents and schools and shelters in
the last town left,
whether to leave or whether to stay,
when to stay is deadly
and to leave is deadly,
and there is literally nowhere to go
for the survivors.

6th September- Undertaking

A task, an undertaking.

A laborious work, a duty.

To find words, to force letters

On the page.

To scream, to cry.

To see things,

Unbearable.

To say things,

Unbelievable.

To fill the page,

Unshakable.

In times of the unspeakable.

To breathe in pain.

And breathe out words.

When words are too weak,

Too fragile to hold.

When breathing is a task.

An undertaking.

Such is a duty to practice,

Daily.

9th August

Bless the belief in survival
of something.
Bless the tenacity of spirit.
Bless those working in
hope,
still writing, teaching, tending, feeding, clothing, reporting
even though it's too late for life,
even though the darkness overwhelms.
Bless the belief in mercy.

25th July- End of humanity

He walks proud and victorious

Spitting lies after lies

'Give us the weapons

We'll finish the job'

A war criminal in their grand room

Surrounded by zombies of shared values

Applauding the use of their weapons

Celebrating the death of moral lessons

They cheered monstrously

As their bombs finish a death camp

Declaring the end of humanity

Under the rubbles of Gazaa

30th September

*The Wicked brag that they
order war crimes like
room service from United Nations.
The Wicked are soaked in
the blood of the innocent
they are drunk on their violent power.*

*The Hannibal Directive
The Dahiya Directive*

*And The Spineless wring their
even more powerful hands.* [10]

---

10 https://x.com/thecradlemedia/status/1839710538852405596?s=46

30th July- A child's head

My son is white with short hair
Did you see his head?

My son is a child with a happy face
Did you see his head?

My son is kind with a bright mind
Did you see his head?

My son just had water with a hug
Did you see his head?

My son is a body with a missing head
Did you see his head?

Are you keeping your head
Looking at a child with no head?

Breathe

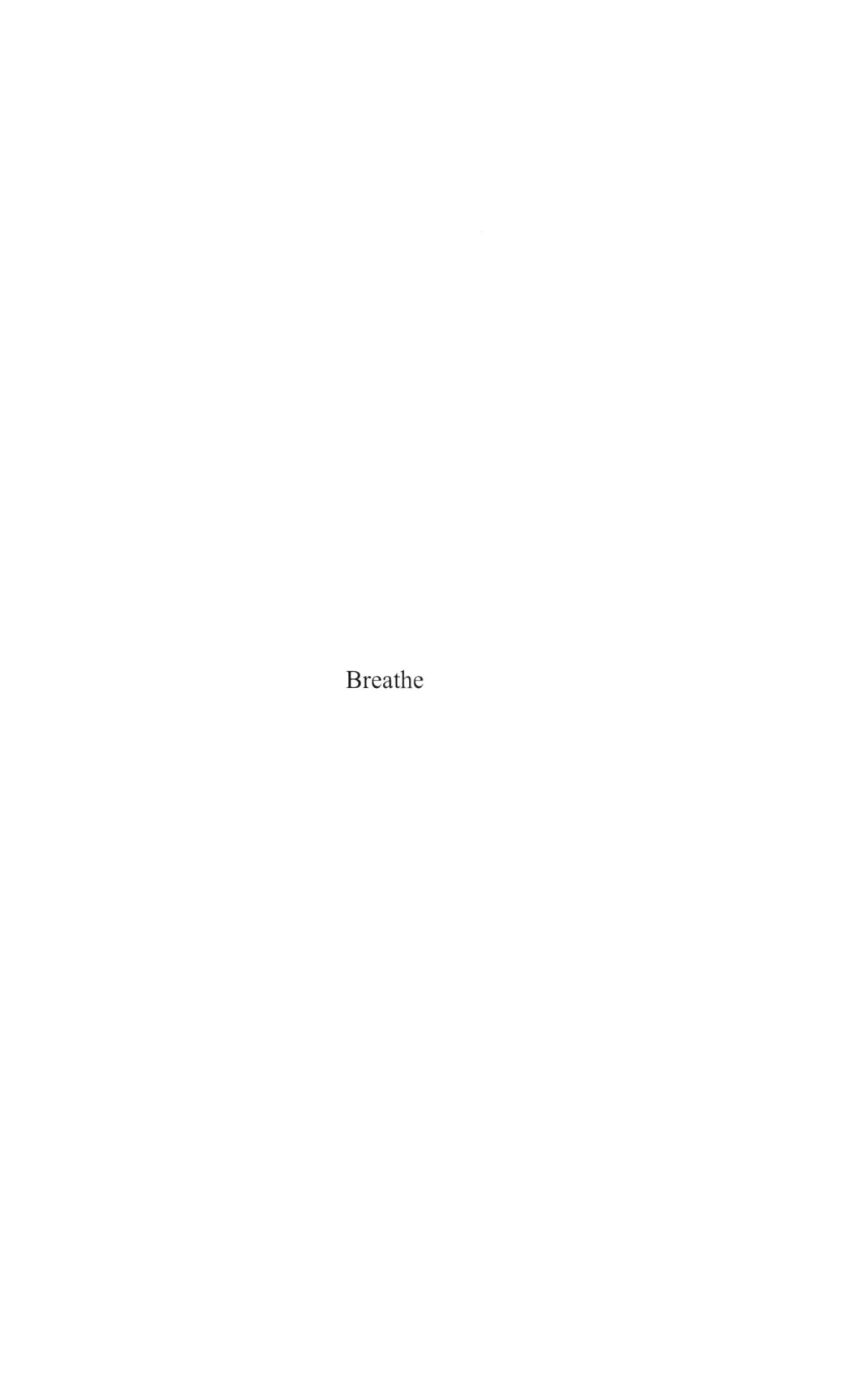

6th September

We will issue orders.
we will call them many names
like 'evacuation'
and 'relocation'
to 'humanitarian zones,'
where we will fire on tents.
There are no red lines
say The Wicked.
Really we are ethnic cleansing; expelling;
terrorising, ignoring the law.

What we want is your land.

27th July- A dad's letter

I tried to look after you, protect you, hide you

I ran between places and tents with you

I held you as you were dying to save you

I rushed you to a hospital but you died; you

Tell God about everything my darling you

You've learned to say it all from you

As I sit by the cold lifeless you

I breathe remembering you

19th July- The sea.

Have you seen our street?

I can't guide my feet

Our maps have no roads

The wicked drop horror that explodes

All I see are piles on top of piles

Ruins, scattered limbs and stolen lives

Look! I think I can see the sea

How far was our house from the sea?

7th August- Gaza sea.

O Gaza sea! What have you seen?
Have your waves echoed our pain?
Your angry flow they can't contain
Pass our cries! Try not to go insane

O Gaza sea! What have you seen?
You witnessed death under the rubble
You saw how we cry and crumble
Our heavy hearts burst like a bubble

O Gaza sea! What have you seen?
Wake the rest of the Mediterranean
Scream and don't mind being alien
I hear you. Your pain is Palestinian

O Gaza sea! What have you seen?
No ebb, no tide, no moon to intervene

12th July

Our bombs are controlled by
Lavender.
It's what we call the system
that turns you, your loved ones, your neighbours
all inhabitants
into unburied, rotting flesh,
which our tanks crush.
Those unbombed, we will starve,
slowly, in a forever war
with impunity.

28th July- A bombed school

Here were happy children in uniform
Learning words about the world

Here they had classes that were warm
Children and songs loudly heard

Here they were learning about rights
Listen! I can hear dreamy noises

Bomb
Bomb

Here is a school among the bombed sites
Bodies, blood, parts and no choices

Here are screams and scattered parts
Scary white bags in a world gone wild

Here are too many grieving hearts
And the whispers of a dying child

19ᵗʰ August

Precision killings
say the leaders of the most moral army in the world.
We will now precisely shoot the horses
who will deliver grain,
telling you that the horses are 'human shields'
made to pull carts in place of amputees,
by Hamas.

Forgive us our sarcasm.
We are weary of your lies.

23rd August- Death calls

A private number on his screen

A call unleashing death threats

Move now or else

Run now or else

A language of cruelty

A tone of inhumanity

A passion for suffering

A mastery for torture

And he rejects the call

He walks back to the tent

And with a shrug he asks:

Isn't death kinder than this life?

17th August

*Bless the family of the
wee boy, if they are still alive
for they did what no one
should have to do in their grief.
They found the 4 pieces of his body
and placed them in a shroud.
There has been no mercy
there are no red lines other than those
on the corpses of the 40.000 dead.*

24th August- Bread

The uneaten bread

The absence of bread

The massacre of the bread

The soaked in blood bread

The mixed with sand bread

The made with animal feed bread

The killed while trying to get bread

The scattered around the dead bread

The dying who waited for some bread

The eaten without any surviving family bread

The buried with a hand holding crumbs of bread

20th September

The Wicked have tested the limits
of the grand words spoken
by the guardians of the grand words
and found that there is no limit
to the wickedness
they might entertain.

5th August- Fire

They set tents on fire

Children burning in fire

Parents screaming 'fire, fire'

They set land on fire

Trees burning in fire

Livelihood eaten by fire

They set life on fire

No water to stop the fire

Conditions of life on fire

22nd August

For those whose teeth were broken.
For those who were beaten.
For those who were raped.
For those set upon by dogs.
For those set upon by rats.
For those electrocuted.
For those whose ears bleed from the loudest music.
For The Wicked who tell of the horrors they perpetrated.

6th August- Scream

And after a loud explosion

A man runs to a massive pile

Shouting out names

Searching for signs of life

Under the rubble he hears a scream

One that restores hope

Yet rips him apart-

Someone is alive, still

The rubble is too heavy to move

As ugly as this world

He only has bare hands

Cracking with blood

And the scream is going low

I can't hear you, the man says

Please say something, he pleas

The scream is gone

16th July

We do not respect rules of war,

say the Wicked.

We will use our precision bombing

to destroy the head quarters

of the United Nations Relief and Works Agency.

There must be no relief.

There must be no works.

We do not respect The Rome Statutes

or Geneva Convention or your pleading. [11]

---

11 https://x.com/unrwa/status/1812841896936366454?s=46

29th August- Lies of defence and security

And they kill and kill

With complete impunity

Laughing at everyone

Destroying everything

Bragging about their crimes

Grabbing more land

Causing endless death

Leaving countless losses

Suffocating the earth

Among lies of defence and security

28th September

How to honour the dead

when the bodies arrived

unannounced?

Unidentified.

Unidentifiable.

Piled in blue bags in an articulated lorry.

No name.

Just numbers.

For dumping on the besieged.

To refuse the undignifying of the dead

is all that remains. [12]

---

12 https://aje.io/jy7uw6

31st August- Little brother

Hey little brother

Why did you go?

We played together

You promised you'll grow

My eyes I can't believe

The wicked forced your soul to leave

Your face looks calm

Your hands feel cold

Your eyes look dreamy

Your lifeless sleep scares me

Look! I found some bread

Stop being hungry and dead

13th July

You must evacuate.

You must take the safe route.

There are snipers who will shoot you.

And we will send quadcopters.

And we will crush with tanks.

And we will starve you.

There is no where to run to but we will

make you run

on your leg that we have not yet amputated.

Say the wicked. [13]

---

13 https://x.com/un_news_centre/status/1811765795413770483?s=46

21st August- O Gaza

O Gaza!

Trapped in the nonbeing zone

Where everyone is spare

And everything can go

Life continues as 'normal'

O Gaza!

Killed by international weapons

Filmed for all to see

But kept under evil covers

Hush! We are neutral as you see

O Gaza!

Days leak into endless death

People, once friends, just leave

Days and people spin in a circle

Too empty and nothing holds

27th August

The wicked knock on the roof.

They say leave your home.

Your ripening dates.

Your old photographs.

We will still attack you in the streets.

Or in your makeshift tent.

And when amputating your limbs

we will tell you to run

from the last hospital.

Our wickedness will know no end.

22nd August- Letdown

Death zones are spreading

Gaza is quickly dying

'Goodbye' is mixed with 'see you'

'Take care' is mixed with 'forgive me'

'Love you' is mixed with 'watch out'

Not knowing which withstands

Between holding and letting go

No time for crying

Only running from bombs

Perhaps walking till death

An old man announces:

'I want to die walking'

He carries a bag

As heavy as life

He holds a heart

As big as the skies

In his eyes a tear sits

Twinkling as the sea

And in his voice cracks

the letdown of a lifetime

5th August

For those displaced four, five, six times.

For those injured four, five, six times.

For the hands that makeshift shelters.

For the hands that makeshift dressings.

For the hands that makeshift stretchers.

For the homes that makeshift homes.

For the hearts that makeshift peace.

1st September- Gaza in September

after Mahmoud Darwish

As you go to school, think of Gaza

As you pack lunches, think of Gaza

As you return to work, think of Gaza

As you fill water bottles, think of Gaza

As you walk with children, think of Gaza

As you hear children laughing, think of Gaza

As you pass a buzzing school, think of Gaza

As you see children in uniform, think of Gaza

As you talk about your holiday trips, think of Gaza

As you see teachers in playgrounds, think of Gaza

As you hear about rights and morals, think of Gaza

As you see who refuses to see Gaza, think of Gaza

2nd August

Bless the birds who stopped singing.

Bless the date palms.

Bless the endangered witnesses.

Bless the strangers at the gate.

Bless the widow.

Bless the orphan.

Bless the unnamed corpse under rubble.

Bless the peace-makers.

Bless the faith in the just world to come.

7th September- The Edge

A civilian population.

Trapped, starved.

Bombed, shredded.

Set on fire,

Pieces in bags.

Remains in a bucket.

Screams in the air.

Smoke in the lungs.

Holes in the hearts.

Utterly dehumanised.

Pushed into the zone,

The non-being space.

Where children are spare,

And nothing matters.

Pushed to the edge,

Of a broken world.

Between the jaws of death,

Under the fall of bombs,

Where birds can't sing,

And trees just bend.

Such is life in Gaza, daily.

8th September- In our millions

A protest, a call.

A demand, a plea.

A moral obligation.

A human wave, a collective.

A global movement,

For justice and peace.

A global movement,

Teaching hope.

Practicing care.

Remaking life,

Amid the ruins.

In our millions,

Against the silence,

The hidden consent,

The claims of neutrality,

The masks of professionalism.

In our millions,

Honouring, mourning.

Remembering, chanting.

Bearing witness.

Naming the world,

As it is.

As it is.

While holding a photo,

A memory of a smiling face.

A shredded child,

Collected in a rice bag.

7ᵗʰ September

And yet the few who spoke out,

Become more,

Become many,

Become a movement for peace,

A river of solidarity,

Finding a flow towards justice.

Tenacious.

Confident.

Righteous.

Sure.

4th October

Bless those who do not kill.
Bless those who tell their friends
where they are wrong
and cease pandering to their
false gods of security;
who ensure that orphanages
are not bombed under a
spurious camouflage
of a 'right to self defence'
with no basis in law.

Bless Those.

4th September- In memory of my brother's friend

I buried my friend's remains

I collected him in a bag

I hugged the bag and cried

I said he was a teacher

I said he was a good man

I said he was my friend

No, he IS my friend

Now he is in this bag

Now he is everywhere,

My brother tells me

9th Sep- Radical love

To love the land,

Even when it's burnt.

To love freedom,

Even when it looks impossible.

To love justice,

Even when it's far away.

To love the old house,

Even when it's just rubble.

To love the olives,

Even when they are weeping.

To love Zaatar,

Even when its smell hurts.

To love kindness,

Even when brutality is the norm.

To love patience,

Even when your pain is unbearable.

To love love,

Even when you are in pieces.

To love hope,

Even when you expect betrayal.

Such is to practice love.

In a loveless world,

Daily.

13th August

Shame is ours
for we have destroyed
so many lives,
with such indiscriminate
bombing of schools and shelters,
that the only way you know
how many we murdered,
is by weighing 70 kilogrammes of body parts.
We must turn from this wickedness.'

This is what the Wicked do not say.

26th August- Calls under bombs

Habibti, dad says, don't you cry

We'll meet one day. We'll try

When earth closes, look at the sky

I hear bombs and I can't reply

I hold my breath and hide a sigh

My voice cracks before I say bye

And now I can't keep my eyes dry

Pain everywhere: so wide, so high

Salam to Gaza, I whisper in reply

11ᵗʰ September

In the ecosystem of genocide
Now The Wicked are tarmacking
new roads on land they have stolen
for their next vile purposes.
It is against the law,
but meeting only
ineffectual rhetoric
of caution.
The Wicked laugh,
emboldened.

Under the tarmac
Blood.

10th September- Unjoinable

And this amputated heart,

Beats to join the unjoinable.

Parallel worlds,

One erasing the other.

And this amputated heart,

Jumps to bear the unbearable.

Endless horrors,

More bodies under the rubble.

And this amputated heart,

Bleeds to speak the unspeakable.

Vulnerable words,

Forcing space for Gaza.

Interrupting. Reminding.

Connecting. Remembering.

Losing. Losing.

As life goes on.

Such is a state of being,

Unsettled. Stunned.

Holding Gaza,

Daily.

7th August

We will send you 89 people.

They will be entirely decomposed.

They will be unidentifiable.

We will supply no details.

You will bury them in a mass grave.

No one will know who they are.

Maybe we dug up a cemetery.

Maybe we tortured them to death.

say the wicked

They were people who were loved. [14]

---

14 Israel returns 'decomposed' bodies of 89 Palestinians to Gaza https://www.aljazeera.com/news/2024/8/5/israel-returns-decomposed-bodies-of-89-palestinians-to-gaza

17th September

The silence is a curse.

It is lazy.

It is the queasy refusal to do the moral work.

It hides behind the camouflage of superficially not understanding.

It stops learning at the deepest levels.

THIS is the moral question Gaza has presented.

It's not complicated. It's hard.

15th September- A curse

Your silence is a curse,

Dropped on the already dead,

And those slowly dying,

And those defending the dead.

Your silence is a curse,

Dropped on Gaza in rubbles,

Schools with no children,

And land deprived of life.

Your silence is a curse,

Dropped on decades of struggle,

Order of laws, rights and freedoms,

And language we used to believe.

Your silence is a curse,

Dropped on own trustworthiness,

Claims of respecting equality,

And words on fighting racism.

22ⁿᵈ September

The Wicked are drunk on their power.

They are drunk on their fear.

They praise their supposed sophistication.

They tout their new cyberwares

with maiming and blood

They become ever more wicked,

determined to make everyone who begs for

a red line, into a terror target

for their evil acts.

11th September- No title

Remains in buckets

Bodies in bags

A child in a rice bag

Pink roller skates

Like an earthquake

Bombed schools

Hospitals in rubble

Erased neighbourhoods

Tents on fire

Bombed refugee camps

Shrinking humanitarian zone

Death blocks

Missing heads

Amputated limbs

Collected body parts

Buried alive

Run over by a tank

Died of forced hunger

Trapped population

Torture camps

The flour massacre

Hanging dead children

Injured child, no surviving family.

A live-streamed genocide

Horrors upon horrors,

Daily.

11th August

Killed.

Murdered.

Assassinated.

Tortured to death.

Bleeding out.

Untreated.

No medicines.

Doctors murdered.

Starving to death.

Illegally.

By the apartheid state.

These are the words we repeat

for ten months,

and 76 years.

15th July- He can hear you

Your son is dead, says a crying man

I'm holding his head between my hands

You're trapped in the north

Your son is killed in the south

Squares of death

Running from death to death

I'm putting the phone next to his ear

Come on, say goodbye to him

He can hear you

Say goodbye

Your son is dead

Say goodbye

8th July

"Run" say the commanders

To the East.

"Run" they roar again.

"Run" "We will obliterate

everywhere you have called home.

Again and again."

"You will have no homes

No food. No water. No hospitals.

No one to document and tell.

"Run. There is nowhere to go."

14th August- Birth certificates

He left his twins to get birth certificates

To document their names

To show their date of arrival

To mark his fatherhood

While away they were bombed

At four days of age

At the edge of time

At the expiry date of birth certificates

He held the papers in disbelief

With grief that cracked his soul

With the maddest of eyes

With the fastest of hearts

He screamed till the stretch of breath

While the world is watching

While weapons are still shipped

While business continues as 'normal'

13th September

Bless the hands digging through sand

after Israel's blast.

Bless the hands that turn the tourniquet

on severed limbs.

Bless the hands trembling showing this

horror upon horrors to the world. [15]

---

[15] https://twitter.com/Shepherds4Good/status/1833293928121909599/video/1

15th August- Little one

Goodbye little one

Your legless body

Once hanging on a branch

Is resting in a box

On top of a red sheet

Without your legs

Your face is beautiful, little one

Look! They found your legs

Both of them

They placed them in the box

Goodbye, little one

You were buried whole

Whole but not one piece

And my heart is never whole

23rd July- Dad's shoes

A child in tears

Wailing

Hugging the shoes

Of his dead dad

During a prayer

Before the burial

Of his murdered father

A child in tears

Screaming

'May God bless

The soul of my baba'

As people gather

To soothe a bit of pain

When no words can heal

A child in tears

Hugging

Holding the shoes that remain

As witness to this cruelty

A memory of a loving dad

A reminder of what happened

And the world comes to a halt

31ˢᵗ August

There are no lines

no red, green, blue,

black, or white lines.

The annihilations we plan

we will practice in the north,

in the south,

in the east,

in the west.

Because we can

and we know

we will never be stopped.

No one with power

to stop us

has proved unfaithful.

say The Wicked

29th July- His face

He buried his children and cried

Looked at the camera, walked aside

His face said it all

He kneeled to pat on the grave

Didn't bother about not being brave

His face said it all

He sat on the ground, turned around

Dried his tears, refused to make a sound

His face said it all

He had the saddest looks, the maddest eyes

Left on his own to memories and cries

His face said it all

11ᵗʰ July

They kill you if you move.

They kill you if you don't.

There is no way out.

They starve you til all systems collapse.

The ICJ ordered an end to this twice.

They do not rest.

They find many ways of violating those Orders.

Many violent ways. [16]

---

16 https://x.com/ajenglish/status/1811119833779429853?s=46

2nd September- To try again

To rebuild a bombed hospital

To mark the reopening day

To remake life amid death

To return to the land still

To practice radical love

To attend to the sick

To come again

To keep trying

In a death camp

29th September

Bless those who hold what remains:

In their horror,

In their rage,

In their betrayal,

In their grief.

Bless the one holding his daughter's sandal.

Bless the one holding the leg of her son.

Bless the one sitting on the rubble of home.

10th July- I cannot

The wicked killed the soul of his soul

Covered in blood and tears

I cannot handle this

I cannot, cries a father

Giving a final hug

Mourning a child's death

Marking a child's short life

Declaring the end of all life

Snatched by evil

Killed in cold blood

Murdered with impunity

Sponsored by your government

I cannot, he says

I cannot, he screams

I cannot, he surrenders

I cannot; I stare and weep

23rd July

"The wicked shredded children,"

Says the Doctor.

"They melted families in front of children.

They incinerated children,' he says.

How do you measure the wounds?

I cannot even measure my own.

I have never seen so many wounded and dead children."

Justice must come quickly [17]

---

17 https://x.com/nour_odeh/status/1815435046301348264?s=46

12th September- Teachers

They killed teachers.

Like many of us.

Like many of us.

Teacher who met to plan.

To remake education,

From the rubble.

Like many of us.

Except;

There was something wrong.

More than one thing:

Wrong side of the border,

Wrong skin colour,

Wrong nationality.

Their DNA can't be rearranged.

Their border can't be lifted.

Their life can't be restored.

Even as they lived

To restore life.

Like many of us,

They were teachers.

They are our teachers now.

Hush! Hush! Hush!

Education, they insist,

Is apolitical.

Leave the baggage.

Leave the news.

Drop the burden!

At the door. Any door.

Just leave!

4th August- Keep telling

O Gaza what is left to say
Yet in silence we can't stay

Your pain filled Earth with grief forever
Screams, death and endless horror

Days bleeds into new days that aren't new
Words tired, eyes sore, voices cracked too

We keep telling, keep witnessing, refusing to stop
Lumps stuck in our throats, as heavy as rock

No end to this telling
No date for this telling

Keep telling
Just keep telling

19th September

Bless those who ensure that
we teach memories of peace.
Bless those whose education is not
education in the memory of violence.
Bless those who teach that history's lessons are
not a security system.
Bless those who uphold and sustain
The real work of peace that brings justice.

4th July- To vote.

When you cast your vote

Think of Gaza

It's not a single issue

It's the web of all issues

When you cast your vote

Think of Gaza

It's not a foreign issue

It's the issue that forces masks to drop

When you cast your vote

Think of Gaza

It's not a Muslim issue

It's the issue staining all humanity

4*th* July

Bless those who do not vote for genocide.

Who know trading arms is not the way.

Who love children everyday, to be raised in peace.

and who know that the dignity of every human is inviolable.

Bless those who vote for a world of justice

and generosity and peace.

10th July

Praise those who love with every fibre of their being.

Praise those who do what no human being should ever have to endure.

Praise those who in deepest distress find love and compassion.

Praise the ones who love after losing everything.

Praise the love that defies evil.

17th July- As I live

I'll keep writing
Forcing sounds
Finding words

I'll refuse numbness
Screaming for Gaza
Speaking about Gaza

I'll feel the pain
Bearing witness
Breaking the silence

I'll stay alive
Feeling for the other
Fighting for humanity

23rd September

Bless the heart break.

Bless the daily struggle

to wake and gather the

Broken pieces of children,

of friends and kin.

Bless with mercy

The daily counting of amputees,

of captives,

of loved ones

under the rubble.

7th October- A Year

It's been a year,

On top of seventy six others.

As long as a lifetime,

With pain, unstoppable.

Fear, unbearable.

Loss, unfathomable.

Among the indescribable.

It's been a year,

Of counting endless death,

With heavy orange nights,

And loud deafening bombs.

Scenes of unimaginable horror,

Pieces in boxes,

Bags and buckets.

It's been a year,

Struggling with words,

Breathing out sounds,

To break the dark silence.

To refuse the indifference.

To stay alive-

Against it all.

7th October

Bless those who know it didn't begin a year ago.

Bless those who mark the many massacres.

Bless those who mourn.

Bless the families of the unheard

under the rubble.

Bless every captive not released

and each one released.

Bless those who struggle for justice

Peace will be theirs.

Khawla Badwan is a scholar of language, education, culture and social justice. She is a Palestinian refugee who lived in Gaza for 14 years.

Alison Phipps is UNESCO Chair in Refugee Integration through Education, Languages and Arts. She has worked with Palestinians in Gaza for 15 years, on projects attempting to sustain a just peace. Her foster daughter was a refugee.

Acknowlegements

We acknowledge the Palestinian struggle of 77 years (and counting). We acknowledge the suffering of the Palestinian people in Gaza whose cries amid the rubble and the flames, with hunger and thirst, under drones and bombs, while covered in mud and blood have taught us what it means to bear witness and to speak of the unspeakable. We grieve with you as we keep telling.

We acknowledge Annick and Sídhe Press for their reaching out and the courage of publishers like Sídhe Press in making room for the cries from Gaza and for the hard consequences they often face.

We also acknowledge artist, Imad Abu Shtayyah, for giving us his permission to use his beautiful artwork- 'we will return', also known as 'we will rise again'- as the cover for our telling of Gaza. We hold Imad's artwork with care, courage and grace.

Thank you to Khawla and Alison for trusting me with their words and their grief.

Thank you to all the journalists in Gaza from whom I have learned so much that I needed to learn– and unlearn. I am so sorry the world has failed you.

Thank you to Jane, Ankh, JP, A. for the love. K. for the support.

*

When life throws a gift

A starlight,

An embrace

A form of endurance.

When life says it's tough.

Here's a gift,

A kinship,

A healing bond,

A team.

Khawla Badwan, October 2024

Printed in Great Britain
by Amazon